I0797353

People in Our Government
Mayor
Linda Hopkins
CITY HA
LIGHTBOX
openlightbox.com

Go to
www.openlightbox.com
and enter this book's
unique code.

ACCESS CODE

LBXE9297

Lightbox is an all-inclusive digital solution for the teaching and learning of curriculum topics in an original, groundbreaking way. Lightbox is based on National Curriculum Standards.

STANDARD FEATURES OF LIGHTBOX

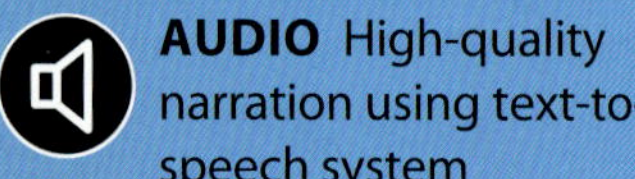

AUDIO High-quality narration using text-to-speech system

ACTIVITIES Printable PDFs that can be emailed and graded

SLIDESHOWS Pictorial overviews of key concepts

VIDEOS Embedded high-definition video clips

WEBLINKS Curated links to external, child-safe resources

TRANSPARENCIES Step-by-step layering of maps, diagrams, charts, and timelines

INTERACTIVE MAPS Interactive maps and aerial satellite imagery

QUIZZES Ten multiple choice questions that are automatically graded and emailed for teacher assessment

KEY WORDS Matching key concepts to their definitions

Contents

Who Is the Mayor?

Almost all cities and big towns in the United States have a mayor. A mayor is the head of **municipal** government. There are more than 19,000 mayors in the United States.

The first mayor to be **elected** in the United States was Cornelius Van Wyck Lawrence. He became the mayor of New York, New York, in 1834. Before then, mayors were **appointed** by the state governor.

Cornelius Van Wyck Lawrence was the mayor of New York for three years.

The Government

A municipal government is led by the mayor and the **council**. Both the mayor and the council are chosen by the people. There are different types of municipal government structures.

The mayor runs the city. He or she meets with city residents to learn what they want their city to be like. The mayor then uses this information to make plans for the city.

The mayor and council meet regularly to make decisions about the city.

Sample Structure of Municipal Government

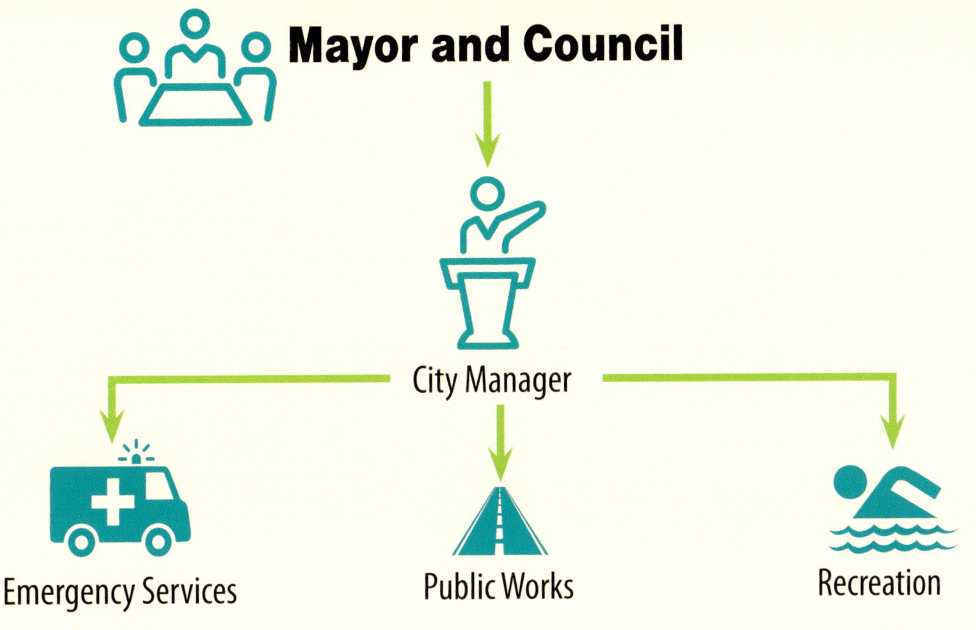

The Role

A mayor is responsible for deciding how to spend the city's money. This means he or she must think about the future of the city and what will help it best. A city may need road repairs, new schools, or more firefighters. Some mayors have the power to make decisions on their own. Other mayors need the council to agree with those decisions before they can be put into action.

Fiorello La Guardia was the mayor of New York City from 1934 to 1945. He asked the **federal** government for money to help the city. La Guardia used this money to build new parks, schools, swimming pools, and hospitals around the city.

Mayor Fiorello La Guardia helped break ground when the city started to build the new North Beach Airport in 1937. Today, it is called LaGuardia Airport.

The first U.S. woman to be a mayor was Susanna Salter of Argonia, Kansas. She was elected in 1887.
Fiorello La Guardia was New York City's 99th mayor.
VOTE
Susanna Salter won two-thirds of the votes for mayor during the 1887 election.

After being mayor of Tivoli, New York, Marc Molinaro ran for governor of the state.

What It Takes

Different cities have different rules for being a mayor. Usually, a person needs to be at least 18 years old and live in the city where he or she wants to be mayor. He or she also usually needs to be a registered voter in that city.

Marc Molinaro was 19 years old when he was elected mayor of Tivoli, New York. He became the youngest mayor in the United States. Molinaro was reelected five times.

In 2019, Lori Lightfoot became the first female African-American to be elected mayor of Chicago.

Getting the Job

Cities and towns have their own rules for how often a mayor is elected. Most elect a mayor every four years. Some cities elect a mayor every two years.

1 When a person decides to run for the office of mayor and start a **campaign**, he or she must file an application with the city by filling out a number of forms.

2 The **candidate** must choose a campaign treasurer, who will look after the money for the campaign.

3

The person running for mayor must collect signatures from people who live in the city. The paper that people sign is called a petition. People sign a petition to show their support for the person running for mayor.

4

The candidate meets with community leaders and residents to tell them what he or she will do for the city if elected mayor. He or she tries to win their votes.

5

On Election Day, the residents of the city vote for who they want as mayor. The person who receives the most votes becomes the next mayor.

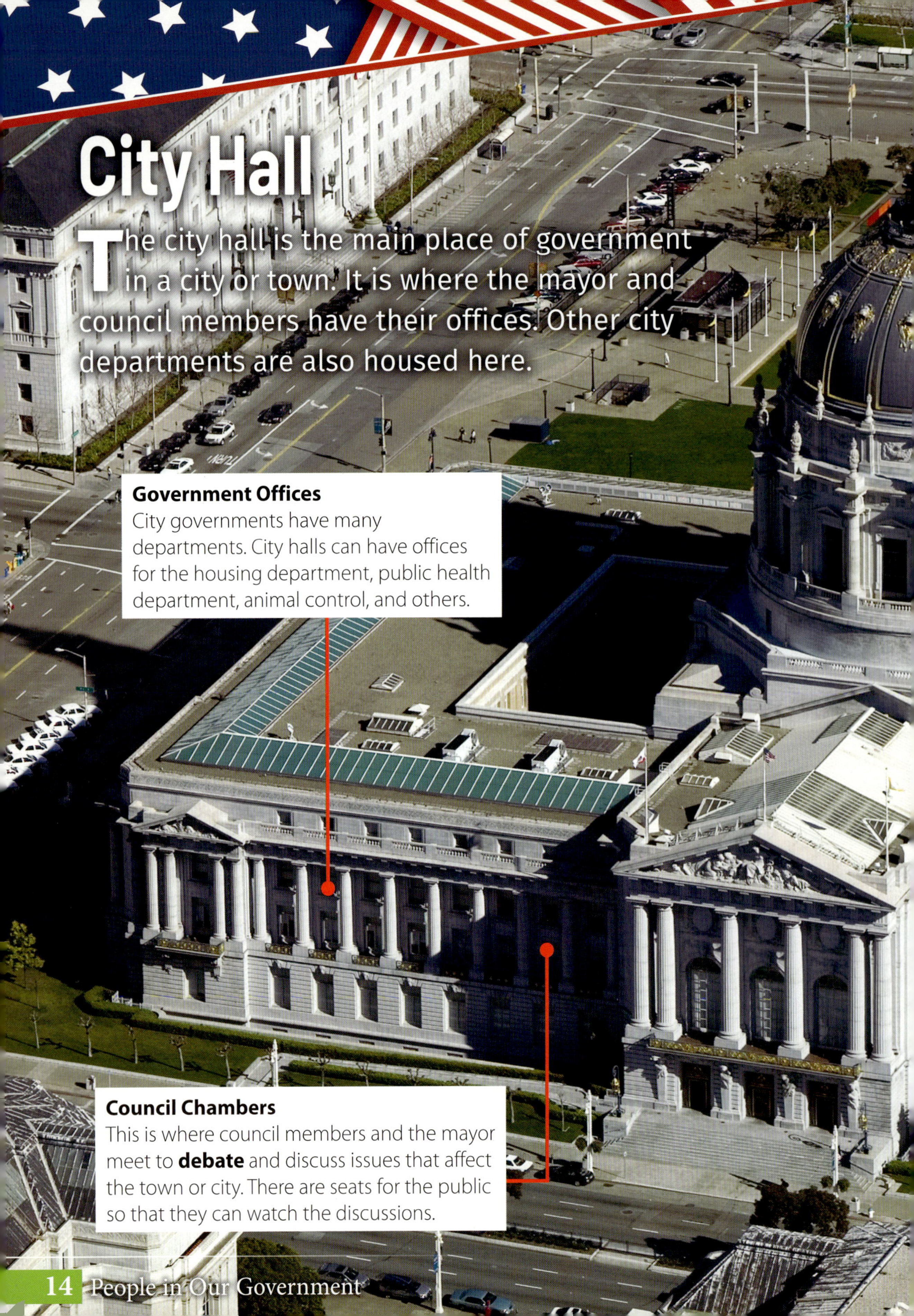

City Hall

The city hall is the main place of government in a city or town. It is where the mayor and council members have their offices. Other city departments are also housed here.

Government Offices
City governments have many departments. City halls can have offices for the housing department, public health department, animal control, and others.

Council Chambers
This is where council members and the mayor meet to **debate** and discuss issues that affect the town or city. There are seats for the public so that they can watch the discussions.

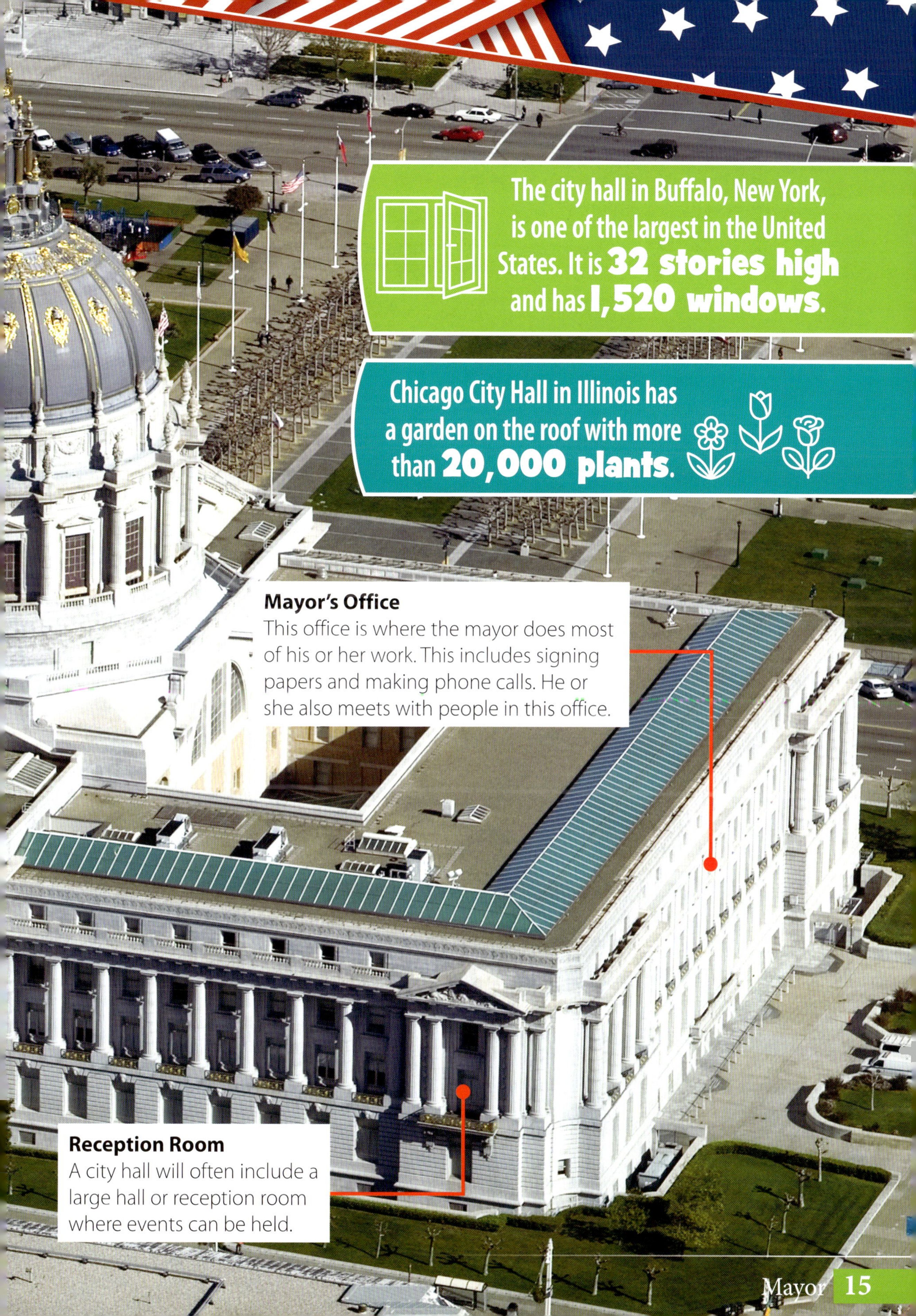

The city hall in Buffalo, New York, is one of the largest in the United States. It is **32 stories high** and has **1,520 windows**.

Chicago City Hall in Illinois has a garden on the roof with more than **20,000 plants**.

Mayor's Office

This office is where the mayor does most of his or her work. This includes signing papers and making phone calls. He or she also meets with people in this office.

Reception Room

A city hall will often include a large hall or reception room where events can be held.

Leading in Public

A mayor's job involves meeting with people in the community. This includes residents, business owners, and workers. The mayor talks to many people in order to make the right decisions for the city.

Different departments, such as finance or public works, share information about the work they are doing during council meetings with the mayor.

Chairs Council Meetings

The mayor is the council meeting **chair**, which means he or she leads the meetings and makes sure that discussions stay on track. Members of the public can watch council meetings.

Attends City Events

The mayor attends events in the city to show support for the local community. He or she sometimes goes to orchestra and theater performances. The mayor also supports local sports teams by watching games.

Mayors walk in holiday parades to meet some of the town's residents.

The mayor attends openings of cultural community centers to make sure those groups feel welcome in the city.

Participates in Ceremonial Events

The mayor is often present when a new building, such as a library or gym, opens in the city. He or she promotes the uses of the new building and how it will benefit the city's residents.

Meets with Business Leaders and the Public

It is important for the mayor to know how people in the city feel about the local government. He or she meets with businesses leaders and the public to hear what they think about their city.

After natural disasters, such as tornadoes, the mayor visits the damaged places and talks to the city residents about their needs.

A Day in the Life

The mayor is the face of his or her city. He or she is the person residents turn to for information about their city. The mayor spends much of his or her time working with others. Mayors have a busy schedule.

Mayors give speeches about new, interesting, and important events and changes happening in their city.

8:00 am The mayor meets with his or her **chief of staff** to go over the events of the day.

9:00 am The mayor attends a **Chamber of Commerce** meeting to hear concerns about business **taxes**.

11:00 am The mayor visits a new school library and reads a story to the third grade class.

1:00 pm The mayor chairs a meeting of the city council where there is a debate about raising city taxes.

4:00 pm The mayor attends a **press conference** to announce a new garbage collection service.

7:30 pm The mayor attends the opening performance of a new theater production.

Notable Mayors

Mayors are remembered for the things they did to make their cities and towns better places to live. Many mayors go on to have other roles in politics. Some have become state governors or worked for the federal government.

CANADA
Wyoming
Nevada
Utah
UNITED
California
Colorado
Arizona
New Mexico
Pacific
Ocean
MEXICO
Texas

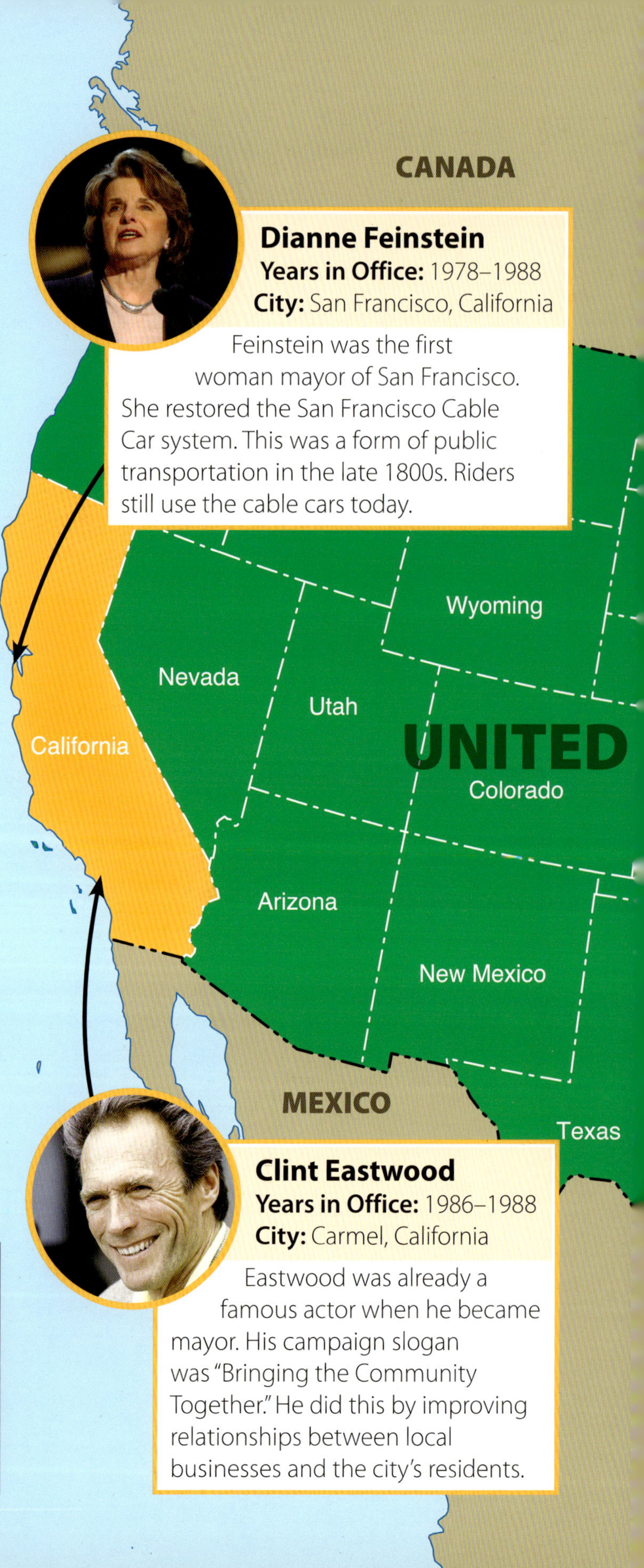

Dianne Feinstein
Years in Office: 1978–1988
City: San Francisco, California

Feinstein was the first woman mayor of San Francisco. She restored the San Francisco Cable Car system. This was a form of public transportation in the late 1800s. Riders still use the cable cars today.

Clint Eastwood
Years in Office: 1986–1988
City: Carmel, California

Eastwood was already a famous actor when he became mayor. His campaign slogan was "Bringing the Community Together." He did this by improving relationships between local businesses and the city's residents.

Hawai'i
Scale
100 Miles
0 100 Kilometers

Alaska
Scale
500 Miles
0 500 Kilometers

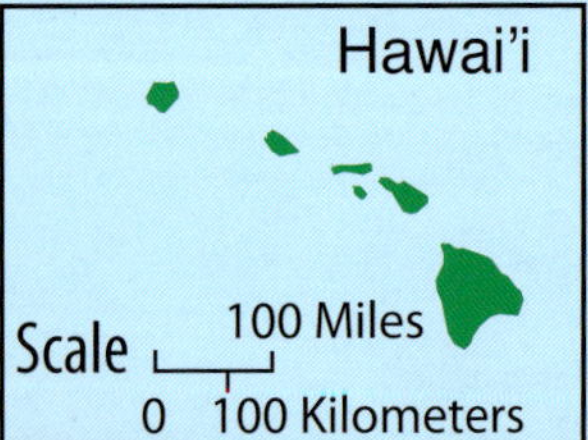

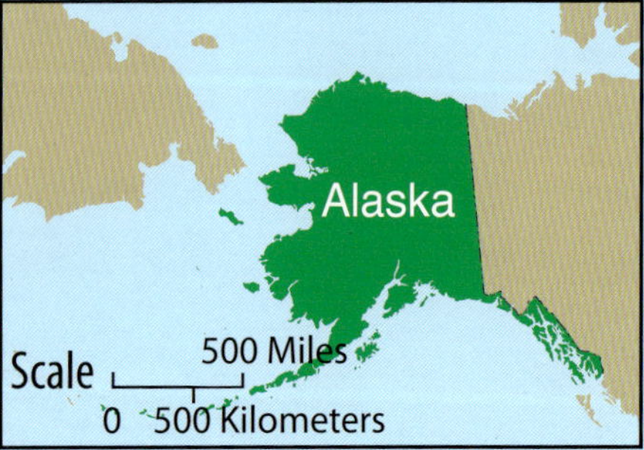

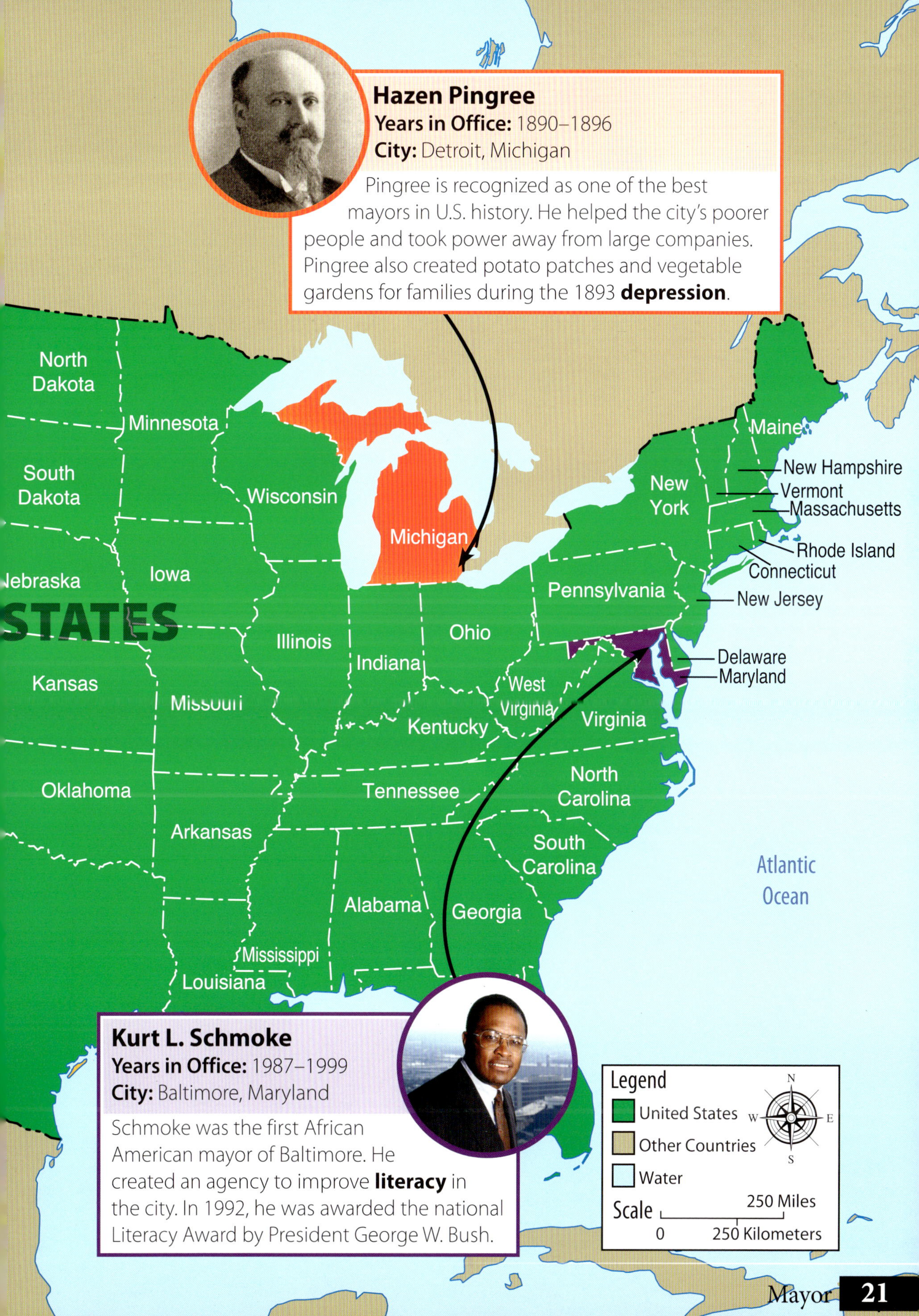

Hazen Pingree
Years in Office: 1890–1896
City: Detroit, Michigan

Pingree is recognized as one of the best mayors in U.S. history. He helped the city's poorer people and took power away from large companies. Pingree also created potato patches and vegetable gardens for families during the 1893 **depression**.

Kurt L. Schmoke
Years in Office: 1987–1999
City: Baltimore, Maryland

Schmoke was the first African American mayor of Baltimore. He created an agency to improve **literacy** in the city. In 1992, he was awarded the national Literacy Award by President George W. Bush.

Quiz

1 Who was the first mayor in the United States to be elected?

2 Who leads a municipal government?

3 When was Fiorello La Guardia mayor of New York City?

4 How old do most cities require mayors to be?

5 What are the ways the mayor leads in public?

6 Which U.S. mayor created potato patches and vegetable gardens for his city?

ANSWERS

1 Cornelius Van Wyck Lawrence **2** The mayor and the council **3** 1934 to 1945 **4** At least 18 years old
5 Chairs council meetings, attends city events, participates in ceremonial events, and meets with business leaders and the public **6** Hazen Pingree

Key Words

appointed: assigned to a specific job

campaign: an effort to become elected

candidate: a person who seeks or is put forward for a job

chair: the person in charge of a meeting or of an organization

Chamber of Commerce: a group that promotes the interests of the local business community

chief of staff: the person at an office or organization who leads the rest of the staff

council: a group of people elected to manage the affairs of a city

debate: a discussion about a subject on which people have different views

depression: a time when there is very little economic activity, which causes unemployment

elected: voted into a job

federal: relating to the national government

literacy: the ability to read and write

municipal: relating to a city or town and its government

press conference: an event organized to provide information and answer questions from the media

taxes: an amount of money that people pay to the government so that it can pay for public services

Index

LIGHTBOX

SUPPLEMENTARY RESOURCES

Click on the plus icon found in the bottom left corner of each spread to open additional teacher resources.

- Download and print the book's quizzes and activities
- Access curriculum correlations
- Explore additional web applications that enhance the Lightbox experience

LIGHTBOX DIGITAL TITLES

Packed full of integrated media

VIDEOS

INTERACTIVE MAPS

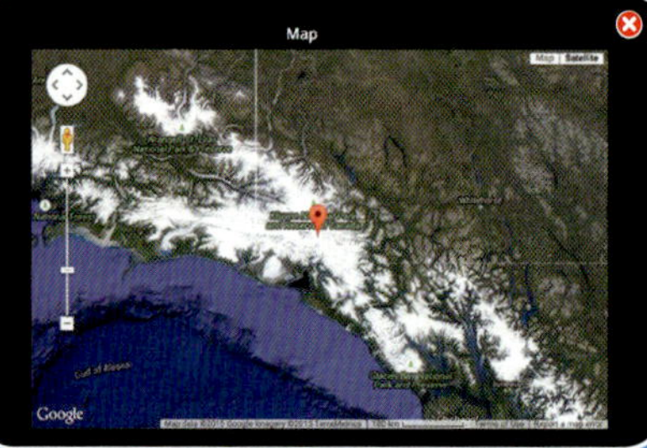

WEBLINKS

SLIDESHOWS

QUIZZES

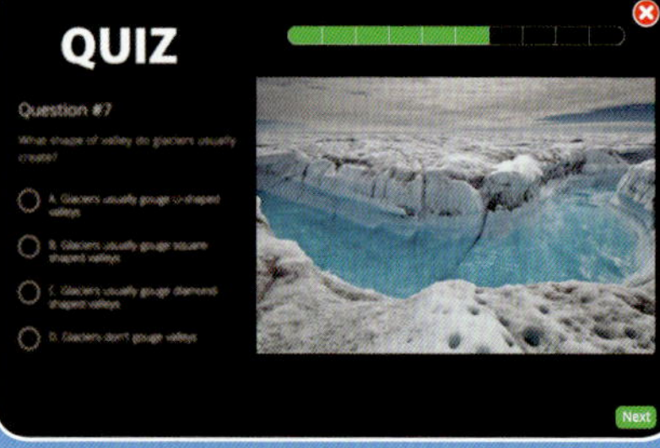

OPTIMIZED FOR

- ✓ TABLETS
- ✓ WHITEBOARDS
- ✓ COMPUTERS
- ✓ AND MUCH MORE!

Published by Smartbook Media Inc.
350 5th Avenue, 59th Floor New York, NY 10118
Website: www.openlightbox.com

Library of Congress Control Number: 2020938414

ISBN 978-1-5105-5452-8 (hardcover)
ISBN 978-1-5105-5453-5 (multi-user eBook)

Printed in Guangzhou, China
1 2 3 4 5 6 7 8 9 0 24 23 22 21 20

062020
111019

Photo Credits
Every reasonable effort has been made to trace ownership and to obtain permission to reprint copyright material. The publisher would be pleased to have any errors or omissions brought to its attention so that they may be corrected in subsequent printings. The publisher acknowledges Alamy, Getty Images, and iStock as its primary image suppliers for this title.

Project Coordinator Heather Kissock
Designer Ana María Vidal